HONOURS

League Champions

1900-01, 1905-06, 1921-22, 1922-23, 1946-47, 1963-64,
1965-66, 1972-73, 1975-76, 1976-77, 1978-7?, 1979-80,
1981-82, 1982-83, 1983-84, 1985-86, 19??-??, 1989-90

European Cup Winners

1976-77, 1977-78, 1980?, ?, 2004-05

FA Cup Winners

1965, 1??, ?86, 1989,
1992, 2001, 2006

League Cup Winners

1980-81, 1981-82, 1982-83, 1983-84,
1994-95, 2000-01, 2002-03, 2011-12

UEFA Cup Winners

1972-73, 1975-76, 2000-01

European Super Cup Winners

1977, 2001, 2005

FA Charity Shield Winners

1964*, 1965*, 1966, 1974, 1976, 1977*, 1979, 1980,
1982, 1986*, 1988, 1989, 1990*, 2001, 2006 (*shared)

Screen Sport Super Cup Winners

1985-86

Division Two Winners

1893-94, 1895-96, 1904-05, 1961-62

Lancashire League Winners

1892-93

Reserve Division One Winners

1956-57, 1968-69, 1969-70, 1970-71, 1972-73, 1973-74,
1974-75, 1975-76, 1976-77, 1978-79, 1979-80, 1980-81,
1981-82, 1983-84, 1984-85, 1989-90, 1999-2000, 2007-08

FA Youth Cup Winners

1995-96, 2005-06, 2006-07

YOU'LL NEVER WALK ALONE

LIVERPOOL
FOOTBALL CLUB

EST·1892

L.F.C.

Road to Kiev 2018

2017/18 was the season Liverpool Football Club returned to Europe's top table. After an eight-year absence, the Reds were back competing in the Champions League and they certainly made an impact. Jürgen Klopp's side blazed a trail across the continent, scoring goals for fun and getting to within touching distance of the most coveted prize. Defeat in the final was ultimately a bitter pill to swallow but the road to Kiev is one that will live long in the memory…

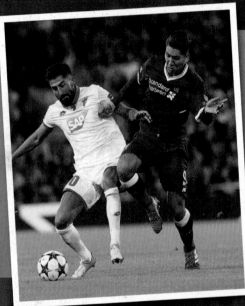

QUALIFIER

TSG 1899 Hoffenheim (a) 2-1
TSG 1899 Hoffenheim (h) 4-2

Liverpool's European campaign began in Germany in mid-August. Simon Mignolet saved an early penalty before Trent Alexander-Arnold smashed home an unstoppable free-kick that set up a crucial 2-1 victory. Three goals inside the first 21 minutes of the return leg a week later put the outcome of the tie beyond doubt. A trip to Kiev in May was far from being contemplated at this stage but the campaign was up and running, with the Reds ready to take their place back among the elite.

GROUP PHASE

Sevilla (h) 2-2
Spartak Moscow (a) 1-1
NK Maribor (a) 7-0
NK Maribor (h) 3-0
Sevilla (a) 3-3
Spartak Moscow (h) 7-0

Liverpool made a tentative start in Group E, drawing their opening two games. A stunning seven-goal demolition of Maribor in Slovenia, however, quickly ignited their charge towards qualification. Amid a further flurry of goals in the remaining three fixtures, top spot was eventually secured with relative ease – courtesy of another 7-0 win at the expense of Spartak Moscow in the final group game.

ROUND OF 16

Porto (a) 5-0
Porto (h) 0-0

Liverpool's hot scoring streak in the group phase certainly didn't go unnoticed across Europe but it wasn't until Porto's previously unbeaten home record was smashed to smithereens that they first began to be spoken about as potential contenders for the trophy. At a rain-soaked Estadio da Dragao the hosts were emphatically swept aside. Sadio Mané grabbed his first hat-trick in a Liverpool shirt and the overall performance of the entire team was one that left even the most experienced observers searching for new superlatives. A goalless draw in the second leg at Anfield mattered little. A serious statement of intent had been issued by the Reds.

Road to Kiev 2018

QUARTER-FINAL

Manchester City (h) 3-0
Manchester City (a) 2-1

Liverpool's Champions League bandwagon was gathering pace but many expected it to come off the rails when the draw for the last eight of the competition paired them with runaway Premier League leaders Manchester City. Even though Liverpool had recently inflicted City's first league defeat of the season, it was Pep Guardiola's team that were still considered to be England's best bet for success in the Champions League. A mouth-watering tie was in prospect and it didn't disappoint. On what was yet another great European night at Anfield, City were completely overwhelmed – by both the power of the crowd and a scintillating first-half display by the Reds. Three goals before the break put them into a virtually unassailable position in the tie and the job was impressively completed with a 2-1 victory at the Etihad in the return leg. Liverpool's credentials in the Champions League were now being extolled and suddenly they were the team to fear.

SEMI-FINAL

AS Roma (h) 5-2
AS Roma (a) 2-4

At one stage during the first leg of this semi-final clash with Roma, Liverpool supporters could have been forgiven for prematurely booking their flights to Kiev. Goals from Mo Salah (2), Sadio Mané and Roberto Firmino (2) saw the Reds race into a barely believable 5-0 lead. With over 20 minutes still left on the clock more goals seemed inevitable. Unfortunately, they came at the opposite end. Two late away goals offered Roma a glimmer of hope and although Liverpool twice led in the second leg, Roma again fought back to ensure a tense finale. Fortunately, their final goal in a 4-2 win came with almost the last kick of the game. Liverpool held on to claim a memorable aggregate victory and, with it, a first appearance in the Champions League final for 11 years, sparking wild celebrations among the jubilant players and travelling supporters.

FINAL

Real Madrid (Kiev) 1-3

45,000 expectant Liverpool supporters trekked across Europe to the capital of Ukraine, hoping to see their beloved team crowned champions of Europe for a sixth time. The Red hordes created a carnival atmosphere in and around the Olympski Stadium but sadly it proved to be a game too far for Jürgen Klopp's team. While Liverpool were viewed as the surprise package of the 2017/18 Champions League season, Real Madrid were the old masters. Twelve-time winners of the competition and aiming to win it for a third successive season, they arrived in Kiev with experience on their side. It may have been Liverpool who ran out winners when the two sides last clashed in European football's showpiece event back in 1981 but 37 years later Los Blancos grasped their chance to finally avenge that defeat. A first-half injury sustained by Mo Salah was a debilitating blow and although Sadio Mané cancelled out Karim Benzema's opening goal, Gareth Bale came off the bench and netted twice to seal Liverpool's fate. Tears were openly shed at the final whistle but it had been a European campaign to be proud of and one that will hopefully provide the springboard for future success.

The KLOPP Report

Ahead of the trip to Kiev in May, manager Jürgen Klopp delivered a brief personal insight into each member of the Liverpool squad that reached the 2018 Champions League final and secured a top four finish in the Premier League…

Jordan Henderson . . . .

The skipper. When he came in he was 25 and already the captain. He's sacrificed himself completely for the team. Has a heart like iron. He's the perfect skipper in the dressing room and in the club, really perfect.

Sadio Mané . . . .

Sadio is obviously a world-class player if he is in his best shape. What a player, huh! Unbelievable.

Dejan Lovren . . . .

The unloved hero. If you had to buy a centre-half with his qualities, that's really big money.

Emre Can . . . .

Physically so strong. And his best skill is he always wants the ball. As a midfielder that's very important.

Danny Ward . . . .

Kind of an old-school British goalkeeper, talking wise. I learned a lot of words just from listening to Wardy during training sessions.

Trent Alexander-Arnold . . . .

That's such a long name I thought I had three players. It was obvious he was a big talent from the first second.

Alberto Moreno. . . . .

An outstanding footballer player. Played a fantastic first part of the season and then he got an injury.

Alex Oxlade-Chamberlain . . . .

I had no clue what a fantastic guy he is. He has world-class potential, there's no doubt about that and he is for sure, already a world-class human being, unbelievable, really funny, really smart.

Dominic Solanke. . . . .

What a start he had when he came in and then he didn't play often. It was so nice to see him score that goal [against Brighton].

Roberto Firmino . . . .

Maybe the inventor of the false nine. A workhorse and the kind of genius technician. You don't have that combination that often.

Simon Mignolet. . . . .

I know it's not easy, the situation, especially with his quality, but he took it really well and pushed Loris on a really high level.

10

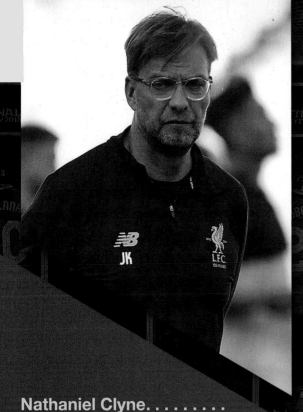

Nathaniel Clyne . . . .

He had his first few minutes in the Champions League against Man City. I did it because I thought he could bring us stability in that moment of the game, so it was really nice.

Adam Lallana . . . .

Most two-footed player I ever saw or had as a player, the movements are just crazy. A real playmaker, a really, really good player.

Joe Gomez . . . .

Very versatile player, very good, very dynamic, very powerful. And for sure, one of the nicest players we have. He will be a fantastic player for us.

Ben Woodburn . . . .

He's still a very young boy, in a really strong football team, but we are very patient and as long as he is patient everything will be fine.

Ragnar Klavan . . . .

He's a genius. Actually, if Ragnar Klavan would believe in himself as much as I believe in him, he would be a world-class centre-half. Simple as that. I think if you gave the boys a choice in training, who do you want to play with, in a five-a-side or whatever – Raggy.

James Milner . . . .

He's a machine Milly, 100 per cent. Fantastic person when he's playing, when he's not playing, he's not. He's a really good player for us, absolutely important.

Joël Matip . . . .

Really funny guy, really funny in the middle of the group. Around training he's not the most chatty person but a really nice boy. Played a big part in our season.

Loris Karius . . . .

He took the chance and made big steps in his development. He was ready and so we let him go, that's it.

Andrew Robertson . . . .

The Scottish car. He's exactly the player we thought he was.

Gini Wijnaldum . . . .

Gini has world-class potential. He is an outstanding football player. A really nice person, constantly smiling.

Danny Ings . . . .

A very good ambassador for a proper English professional in the best way and a top finisher, 100 per cent.

Virgil Van Dijk . . . .

The big man! He's brought a lot of stability and it's really good. Worth each penny we paid.

Mo Salah . . . .

He's so funny as a person, he's a fantastic ambassador for the whole Arabic world, so it's so nice to have him around. What a player!

Domestic Season Review

The 2017/18 season is one that will always be remembered more for what Liverpool achieved in Europe than what they did domestically. Nevertheless, while the Reds lit up the continent, at home they also enjoyed a relatively successful campaign. Participation in the cup competitions fizzled out prematurely and the Premier League title also disappeared from their sights early, yet the goal of a top four finish was always attainable and the chase for it was sustained right to the very end...

AUGUST

12/8/17 – Watford (a) 3-3

19/8/17 – Crystal Palace (h) 1-0

27/8/17 – Arsenal (h) 4-0

Liverpool's Premier League campaign got off to a thrilling, but ultimately disappointing, start. On a sun-drenched Saturday lunchtime at Vicarage Road Mo Salah netted his first goal for the club, but the Reds had to settle for just one point after conceding a late equaliser. Seven days later, Sadio Mané was the match-winner at home to Crystal Palace – a game that saw Andrew Robertson mark his debut with an outstanding performance at left-back, while Liverpool ended the month on a high by scoring four without reply against a shell-shocked Arsenal, then strengthening their ranks with the capture of Gunners midfielder Alex Oxlade-Chamberlain in a pre-deadline day swoop.

SEPTEMBER

9/9/17 – Manchester City (a) 0-5

16/9/17 – Burnley (h) 1-1

23/9/17 – Leicester City (a) 3-2

Early season optimism was punctured in emphatic fashion at the Etihad Stadium. Sadio Mané was harshly sent off and Manchester City fully capitalised as Liverpool crashed to their heaviest defeat in years. A home draw with Burnley the following week did little to lift spirits but a much-needed away win at Leicester, where a Simon Mignolet penalty save proved decisive, thankfully brought this frustrating spell to an end.

CARABAO CUP

3rd round: 19/9/17 – Leicester City (a) 0-2

Liverpool's interest in the Carabao Cup was short and most definitely not sweet. In what was the first of two games in four days at the King Power Stadium, the Reds bowed out at the first hurdle, with second half goals by Ozaki and Slimani condemning them to an earlier than expected exit from the competition.

OCTOBER

1/10/17 – Newcastle United (a) 1-1

14/10/17 – Manchester United (h) 0-0

22/10/17 – Tottenham Hotspur (a) 1-4

28/10/17 – Huddersfield Town (h) 3-0

In the month that Anfield's Centenary Stand was officially renamed in honour of club legend Kenny Dalglish, supporters must have wished that the former number seven could have turned back time and pulled on his boots again. Back-to-back draws and a heavy loss away to Tottenham severely stunted Liverpool's Premier League title aspirations, although October ended on a positive with victory at home to Huddersfield.

NOVEMBER

4/11/17 – West Ham United (a) 4-1

18/11/17 – Southampton (h) 3-0

25/11/17 – Chelsea (h) 1-1

29/11/17 – Stoke City (a) 3-0

Manchester City may have been setting the pace at the top of the Premier League but Liverpool remained in contention with the chasing pack – a position they maintained during November, taking 10 points from a possible 12. Victories over West Ham, Southampton and Stoke were tempered only by a late Willian goal that denied them a deserved victory over reigning champions Chelsea.

DECEMBER

2/12/17 – Brighton & Hove Albion (a) 5-1

10/12/17 – Everton (h) 1-1

13/12/17 – West Bromwich Albion (h) 0-0

17/12/17 – Bournemouth (a) 4-0

22/12/17 – Arsenal (a) 3-3

26/12/17 – Swansea City (h) 5-0

30/12/17 – Leicester City (h) 2-1

High-scoring wins at the expense of Brighton, Bournemouth and Swansea, plus a spirited comeback against Leicester saw the Reds climb back into the top four for the first time since the opening month of the season. Their December points haul, however, could and should have been much better – had they not surrendered a two-goal lead at Arsenal and been held to frustrating home draws by Everton and West Brom.

Domestic Season Review

JANUARY

1/1/18 – Burnley (a) 2-1

14/1/18 – Manchester City (h) 4-3

22/1/18 – Swansea City (a) 0-1

30/1/18 – Huddersfield Town (a) 3-0

2018 got off to the best possible start for Liverpool – with the signing of Virgil Van Dijk and a late Ragnar Klavan winner away to Burnley. Two weeks later the Reds became the first team to inflict a Premier League defeat on runaway leaders Manchester City, emerging victors in a seven-goal thriller at Anfield. A surprise defeat at struggling Swansea drew criticism but normal service was resumed when Huddersfield were beaten comfortably away from home.

FA CUP

3rd round:
5/1/18 – Everton (h) 2-1

4th round:
27/1/18 – West Bromwich Albion (h) 2-3

The opening month of the year also witnessed the start and end of Liverpool's FA Cup campaign. The third round was memorable for the fact that local rivals Everton were beaten and that debutant Virgil Van Dijk headed in a late winner at the Kop end. Struggling West Brom in round four should have been straightforward but with VAR in use at Anfield for the first time, a night of confusion and controversy ended with the Baggies coming from behind to claim a surprise victory.

FEBRUARY

4/2/18 – Tottenham Hotspur (h) 2-2

11/2/18 – Southampton (a) 2-0

24/2/18 – West Ham United (h) 4-1

There was enough drama in the closing stages of the home game with Tottenham to fill an entire campaign. Penalty controversy involving Harry Kane and a goal of the season contender from Mo Salah ensured it finished two-apiece. Once the fall-out subsided Liverpool dusted themselves down and continued their ascent up the table, with routine wins over Southampton and West Ham enough to see them displace Manchester United in second place.

MARCH

3/3/18 – Newcastle United (h) 2-0

10/3/18 – Manchester United (a) 1-2

17/3/18 – Watford (h) 5-0

31/3/18 – Crystal Palace (a) 2-1

Liverpool entered March as one of the form teams in the country but the battle for second place took a pivotal twist in the wrong direction when they went to Old Trafford and lost. On what was a rare off-day for Klopp's side, it was United who regained the ascendancy. Liverpudlian eyes, however, were already becoming fixated on a much bigger prize and the disappointment of defeat was quickly shrugged aside. Winning ways were soon restored as Salah scored four against Watford then hit a late winner at Palace.

APRIL

7/4/18 – Everton (a) 0-0

14/4/18 – Bournemouth (h) 3-0

21/4/18 – West Bromwich Albion (a) 2-2

28/4/18 – Stoke City (h) 0-0

With the Champions League taking centre stage during April, domestic matters took something of a back-seat in terms of importance – even the Merseyside derby at Goodison Park. The subsequent goalless draw was of little concern as the Reds marched on in Europe but vital ground in the Premier League was lost later in the month when relegation threatened West Brom and Stoke emulated the Blues by taking points off the Reds. It meant a top four finish was no longer the certainty it once seemed.

MAY

6/5/18 – Chelsea (a) 0-1

13/5/18 – Brighton & Hove Albion (h) 4-0

Having dropped those unexpected points at the tail end of the previous month, Liverpool's trip to Stamford Bridge on the penultimate weekend of the season took on added importance. Fifth-placed Chelsea were waiting in the wings should the Reds falter and a home win meant the race for fourth place would go down to the wire. For Liverpool, a draw with Brighton would suffice and, although a more important date with Real Madrid loomed, they completed the task with ease, romping to a 4-0 victory to ensure that, no matter what happened in Kiev, the Liver Bird would be flying proud once again in the Champions League the following season.

Welcome to LIVERPOOL

The summer of 2018 was a highly productive one for Liverpool in the transfer market as Jürgen Klopp made four top-class additions to his first team squad…

NABY KEITA
Signed from Red Bull Leipzig

'I like the colour red, it suits me! It is an honour to have this shirt and play for such a huge club.'

What made Liverpool the right club for you to join?
I chose Liverpool because it is a team I watched often – and I also spoke a lot about it with Sadio [Mané]. He told me a lot about the team and the club. I also spoke with the coach, who told me about the project for the team and that motivated me to be here.
What kind of qualities do you hope to bring to Liverpool?
Firstly, I am somebody who plays in a defensive role and we need to start with that, but then I need to bring the ball forward and help the attack. I've always got a desire to win – I believe I'm a winner.
And do you believe there is still room for improvement?
Yes, of course there is. When I see how things have progressed here, I think if I am brave I can do the same and develop further.
You're taking the number eight jersey here – how much of a privilege is that?
Yes, it pleases me a lot. It's an important number and it carries a lot of history – but more importantly for me, having this number gives me the motivation to play and to follow in the footsteps of the players who've worn this shirt before.

FABINHO
Signed from Monaco

'I am really excited about this move. This is something that I always wanted – this is a giant of a team.'

What makes this club so appealing to join?
There are many things. The infrastructure at the club is very good. Also, other players that played here – they only say good things about Liverpool. Liverpool are in a league that is probably the best in the world, so there were many positive points for me to choose to come and I am very, very happy to be here.
How would you describe your own game?
I believe I am a player that can organise the game well for my team. I play with a lot of intensity and I'm quite strong in man-marking. I know that the type of football here is quite intense and physical but I think I got some of that while playing in France and I hope I won't find any problems to adapt to this league.
What are your biggest aims for your time with Liverpool?
I came to Liverpool because I wanted to leave Monaco for an ambitious club, a club that plays to win every competition. Liverpool Football Club is one of these teams. I will try to create my own history at this football club. Hopefully, on a personal level, I'm able to win titles with this club. I will try to grow and learn and improve myself, and to be part of the club's history.

XHERDAN SHAQIRI
Signed from Stoke City

'I just want to say I'm really happy to be here. I hope we can have a lot of beautiful moments in the coming years.'

Why is Liverpool the right club for you?
As a player you always want to be on the biggest stage in football. A few years ago I wanted to come too but it didn't happen. I'm really happy that now I'm finally here. I want to improve myself too, I want to be with the best and I want to win titles. That's what I'm here for.

Do you relish the challenge of getting into the team?
In football there are challenges everywhere. Of course, Liverpool have top players, very good players, young players. It's difficult for everybody. I'm very glad to be here and I believe in myself. The most important thing is to be a team and win as a team. There aren't only 11 players on the pitch; it's more than 11 players who win titles.

Your objective seems to be clear…
Of course. I want to win titles – that's my ambition. I already know how to win from Bayern Munich, we won the treble and it was an amazing feeling. I'm confident we can win a lot of titles. The fans deserve to win titles. Hopefully we have a good season and try to be hungry to win titles.

ALISSON BECKER
Signed from AS Roma

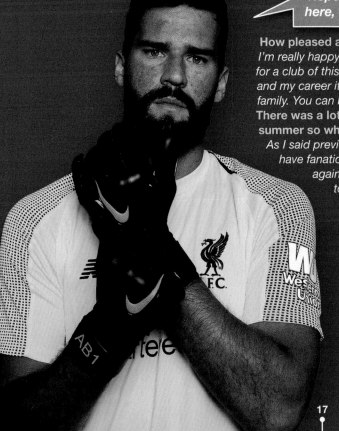

'Hopefully I can play a part in the history being created here, win titles and see Liverpool rise once again.'

How pleased are you to become a Liverpool player?
I'm really happy, it's a dream come true to wear such a prestigious shirt for a club of this size that is used to always winning. In terms of my life and my career it's a huge step for me being part of this club and this family. You can be certain that I'll give my all.

There was a lot of speculation about your future through the summer so why is Liverpool the right club for you?
As I said previously, Liverpool are a team with a habit of winning, that have fanatical fans that are behind the team in every game. Playing against them last year in the Champions League, I was able to experience that atmosphere and that game had an influence on me. I believe this is going to add a great deal to my career in terms of professional growth.

What kind of qualities are you hoping to bring to Liverpool? How would you describe yourself and your style?
I like to show my ability on the field. I'm not one to show off with words. I'm a calm goalkeeper and above all I've got a real desire to win. When I get on the pitch I give everything for the team, everything for the shirt. I look to work on all aspects of my game, always aiming for perfection and looking to improve every day.

Goal Of The Season
2017/18

Liverpool scored an incredible 135 goals in all competitions during the 2017/18 campaign, here are ten of the best...

Mo Salah v Tottenham Hotspur (h)
4 February 2018

Sadio Mané v Burnley (a)
1 January 2018

Mo Salah v Everton (h)
11 December 2017

Roberto Firmino v Manchester City (h)
14 January 2018

Mo Salah v Porto (a)
14 February 2018

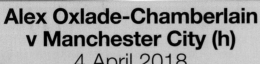

Alex Oxlade-Chamberlain
v Manchester City (h)
4 April 2018

Mo Salah v AS Roma (h)
24 April 2018

Mo Salah v Manchester City (h)
14 January 2018

Trent Alexander-Arnold v Hoffenheim (a)
15 August 2017

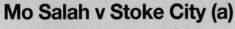

Mo Salah v Stoke City (a)
29 November 2017

Football, of course, is all about opinions, so what would be your top 10 Liverpool goals of the 2017/18 season?...

1	2	3	4	5
6	7	8	9	10

PLAYER PROFILES

ALISSON BECKER

Date of birth: 2/10/1992

Birthplace:
Novo Hamburgo (Brazil)

Squad Number: 13

Did You Know?
Alisson followed in his brother's footsteps in becoming a goalkeeper and actually dislodged him from the number one spot at his first club Internacional

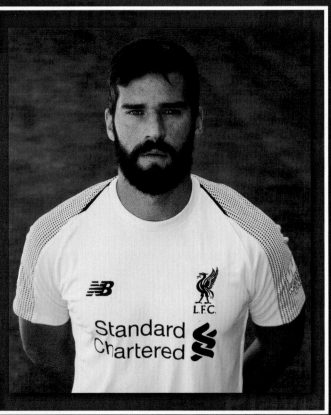

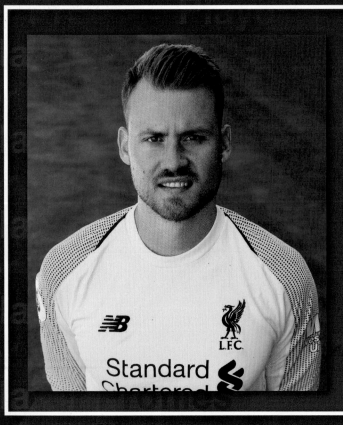

SIMON MIGNOLET

Date of birth: 6/3/1988

Birthplace: St Truiden (Belgium)

Squad Number: 22

Did You Know?
Mignolet enjoyed a dream start to his Reds career by saving a last-gasp penalty on his debut in a 1-0 win against Stoke City in August 2013

TRENT ALEXANDER-ARNOLD

Date of birth: 7/10/1998

Birthplace: Liverpool

Squad Number: 66

Did You Know?
Alexander-Arnold captained Liverpool at under-16 and under-18 level

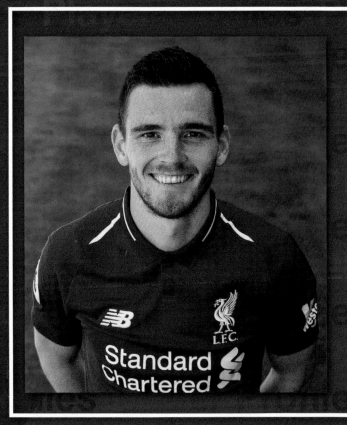

ANDREW ROBERTSON

Date of birth: 11/3/1994

Birthplace: Glasgow

Squad Number: 26

Did You Know?
As a boy Robertson was a fanatical Celtic supporter and season-ticket holder at Parkhead

Have You Met Mighty Red?
Liverpool FC's Official Mascot

MIGHTY RED
LFC OFFICIAL MASCOT

With a total of 14 arm spikes (7 on each arm) and 4 tail spikes, Liverpool's 18 league titles are represented.

Mighty loves wristbands: he wears one with his name on and one with YNWA (You'll Never Walk Alone).

With or without boots, Mighty is great at football but when he wants to look the part, his favourite boots are New Balance.

Mighty's mohawk features 5 head spikes – one for each European Cup success.

When playing football, Mighty loves to wear his Liverpool shirt. It has the number 12 on it, because like all supporters, we are all the twelfth player.

MIGHTY RED'S FAMILY TREE

DAD 'Liverbird' ——— **MUM** 'Motherbird'

ME 'Mighty Red' | **LITTLE SIS** 'Ruby Red' | **BABY BROTHER** 'Little Liver'

Things Mighty Red likes to do...

How to Make Mighty Red Slime

Things you will need:
- 1 cup of PVA glue
- 3/4 cup of shaving foam
- Optrex multi action eye wash
- Red Paint

Method:
Mix 1 cup of PVA glue and 3/4 cup of shaving foam. Slowly add teaspoon at a time of Optrex multi action eye wash and stir.
Stop adding eye wash once the slime is slightly sticky – just a tiny bit sticky!
Then play with in hands until not sticky.
If still a bit sticky add a tiny bit of shaving foam and 2 teaspoons of eye wash!!
(Make as big as you want but use the same ratio)
Keep adding paint until you get the colour you want.

Mighty Red Photo Tick List

- Shankly Statue Selfie
- The Shankly Gates
- Tribute to the 96
- Mighty Red Family Park
- The Kop Singing "You'll Never Walk Alone"
- Main Stand L.F.C. Crest
- Players Entrance
- The Club Shop

ALLEZ ALLEZ ALLEZ!

It became the soundtrack of Liverpool's march to the 2018 Champions League final and it's now firmly established as one of the most popular songs on the Kop.

Since February 2018, 'Allez Allez Allez' has reverberated around every ground and city where the Reds have played.

Sung to the tune of 'L'Estate Sta Finendo' – an Italian disco hit by Righeira in the mid-1980s – it had previously been adopted by supporters at a number of other clubs across Europe, notably Napoli, Porto and Atletico Madrid.

The version that's now ringing in all our ears came about after the lyrics were re-worded by Liverpool fans Phil Howard and Liam Malone. Through the power of social media, and the best efforts of local singer Jamie Webster, who regularly performed it as part of his post-match sets, it gradually morphed into a song that all Liverpudlians latched onto.

But just in case you still don't know all the words, here they are....

**We've Conquered All Of Europe
We're Never Going To Stop
From Paris Down To Turkey
We've Won The Lot
Bob Paisley And Bill Shankly
The Fields Of Anfield Road
We Are Loyal Supporters
And We Come From Liverpool
Allez Allez Allez
Allez Allez Allez.....**

In May 2018 Jamie Webster recorded his version of the song and released it via iTunes and Google, with all proceeds going to An Hour For Others, an Anfield-based charity that supports members of the L4 community in various ways.

The Mo Salah Story
Liverpool's Egyptian King

With a phenomenal 44 goals in his first season as a Liverpool player, it's no surprise that Mohamed Salah became an instant hero among supporters on the Kop. In the months following his arrival from AS Roma during the summer of 2017, Salah went from strength to strength – smashing a multitude of goalscoring records and collecting a glittering array of personal accolades. From Cairo to the Kop, this is his story:

Born on 15 June 1992 in Basyoun, Egypt, football was in Mo Salah's blood from an early age...

I first fell in love with football when I was a kid, around seven or eight years old. I remember watching the Champions League all the time and then trying to be like the Brazilian Ronaldo, Zidane and Totti when playing out in the street with my friends. I loved those kinds of players, players who played with magic.

He showed early promise as a footballer and was soon snapped up by his local club...

It was when I was 14 that I first signed with Arab Contractors (El Mokawloon) and my career in the professional game began – but it was a tough time for me. It was a four to four-and-a-half-hour journey five days a week to get to training. I was having to leave school early to travel to training. I was only at school for two hours a day during that time. For five days a week, every week for three or four years, I would make this journey. Training was always at 3.30pm or 4pm. I would finish training at say 6pm, then I'd go home and arrive at 10pm or 10.30pm. Then it was eat, sleep and then the day after the same thing. If I hadn't become a footballer, I cannot say what I might have become because ever since I started playing at 14, everything in my mind was about becoming a footballer.

That potential was soon fulfilled. He impressed in the Egyptian league and made his senior debut for the national team before joining Basel in 2012...

It was very difficult to move to a club on another continent, especially at such a young age. I was there alone, but all the time I was thinking about improving myself. On the pitch, it was a step up for me. What I can say is Basel is a fantastic club…without Basel I wouldn't be the player I am now. 100 per cent.

After helping Basel to the Swiss title and a place in the Europa League semi-final, his signature was coveted by a number of leading European clubs and in January 2014 he moved to Chelsea…

There was interest from Liverpool when I went to Chelsea, but I think if I'd come at that time maybe things wouldn't have gone as well then as they have for me now. Who knows? I learned a lot from Chelsea; I learned how to be more professional and to become a better person and player. It was a big step in my career. It was while I was at Chelsea that I first got to play at Anfield. I can remember I told myself, 'I have to come here one day and play' after I'd experienced that atmosphere.

First team opportunities were limited at Stamford Bridge and after just six first team starts he went to ply his trade in Italy, first on loan at Fiorentina and then AS Roma...

I had a good four months at Fiorentina. Before I went there, it was very clear in my mind: I deserve to play. I had belief in my ability and I was going to Fiorentina to show everyone my football and what I could do. Then I had a great two years in Rome and I was very, very happy there. I think I changed the perception of me during my time with Fiorentina and then Roma.

Jürgen Klopp was a big admirer and during the summer of 2017 Salah completed his transfer to Liverpool for a club record fee...

I'd said to myself, 'I want to come back to England'. It was always in my mind, coming back here. I wanted to play here and show everyone my football. When I realised I was very close to coming here, I was very, very happy – and after speaking to the boss for the first time after the deal was agreed, I was even happier. Why were Liverpool the right club for me? Because of many things. I even used to play as Liverpool on the PlayStation on FIFA when I was 18 or 19, as Steven Gerrard, Sami Hyypia, Jamie Carragher, Michael Owen and Xabi Alonso. I also remembered that atmosphere again and it came into my mind.

Liverpool's number 11 quickly settled at Anfield and struck up an instant rapport with the Liverpool supporters…

I am happy when the fans sing my name. I can hear them on the pitch and it makes me happy. It makes you feel like, 'wow'. It changes your emotions. I have to thank the fans very much for singing my name. Really, I respect it a lot. It's a big thing for me…to have the fans singing my name every game, showing me love and respect, it means a lot to me.

Salah's first season with the Reds was one to remember and he's optimistic for an even brighter future…

It's going good for me here, but I always felt I would settle quickly. And I think I can get better, 100 per cent. I can improve on many things, so I have to keep working hard, I have to keep looking forward. As a team, I know we haven't won the Premier League for a long time, so I would love to win it with Liverpool. We have a great team, we have a great manager, so everything is good at the club – and I am sure we can win trophies here together.

MO SALAH

The 2017/18 season was a record-breaking season in more ways than one for the Kop's Egyptian King. Here are all his vital facts and stats....

Appearances: 52   Goals: 44

Goals Breakdown

By Competition

Premier League:	32
Champions League:	11
FA Cup:	1

By Minutes

1-15 minutes:	4
16-30 minutes:	7
31-45 minutes:	11
46-60 minutes:	7
61-75 minutes:	4
76-90 minutes:	11

By Opposition

Watford:	5	Roma:	2
Southampton:	3	Spartak Moscow:	1
Manchester City:	3	Porto:	1
West Ham United:	3	Sevilla:	1
Leicester City:	3	Hoffenheim:	1
Tottenham:	3	Brighton & Hove Albion:	1
NK Maribor:	3	Crystal Palace:	1
WBA:	2	Huddersfield Town:	1
Stoke City:	2	Newcastle United:	1
Bournemouth:	2	Chelsea:	1
Arsenal:	2	Burnley:	1
		Everton:	1

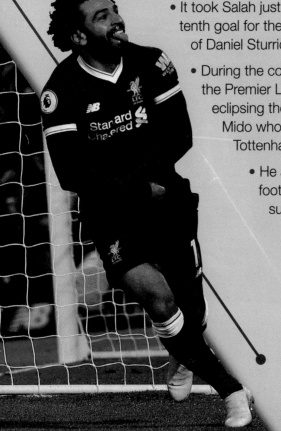

- It took Salah just 13 games to register his tenth goal for the Reds, equalling the record of Daniel Sturridge

- During the course of the season he became the Premier League's top scoring Egyptian, eclipsing the record set by fellow countryman Mido who netted 22 for Middlesbrough, Tottenham and Wigan between 2004 and 2010

- He also became the scorer of most left-footed goals in a Premier League season (24), surpassing fellow Anfield icon Robbie Fowler

- Among his incredible 44-goal haul was one penalty (away to Huddersfield) and a hat-trick (home to Watford), while just two of his goals were scored after coming on as a substitute (both away to Stoke)

- Salah is second only to Ian Rush (47) as the scorer of most Liverpool goals in a single season

Record Breaker

Most Liverpool Goals in a debut season

Mohamed Salah	44	2017/18
Fernando Torres	33	2007/09
Kenny Dalglish	31	1977/78
George Allan	28	1895/96
Albert Stubbins	28	1946/47
Tony Hateley	27	1967/68
Fred Pagnam	26	1914/15
John Miller	25	1892/93
Jimmy Smith	23	1929/30
Roger Hunt	23	1959/60
Dean Saunders	23	1991/92

Most Liverpool Goals in a Premier League season

Mohamed Salah	32	2017/18
Luis Suarez	31	2013/14
Robbie Fowler	28	1995/96
Robbie Fowler	25	1994/95
Fernando Torres	24	2007/08
Luis Suarez	23	2012/13

Most Premier League goals in a 38-game season

Mohamed Salah	32	2017/18
Alan Shearer	31	1995/96
Cristiano Ronaldo	31	2007/08
Kevin Phillips	30	1999/2000
Thierry Henry	30	2003/04
Robin Van Persie	30	2011/12
Didier Drogba	29	2009/10
Harry Kane	29	2016/17
Thierry Henry	27	2005/06
Sergio Aguero	26	2014/15

Top Premier League Goalscorers 2017/18

Mohamed Salah	32
Harry Kane	30
Sergio Aguero	21
Jamie Vardy	20
Raheem Sterling	18
Romelu Lukaku	16
Roberto Firmino	15
Alexandre Lacazette	14
Gabriel Jesus	13
Eden Hazard	12

The Champions League may have agonisingly evaded his clutches but in terms of individual accolades, Salah swept the board in 2017/18…

- PFA Player of the Year
- FWA Footballer of the Year
- Premier League Player of the Season
- Liverpool Player of the Season
- Liverpool Players' Player of the Season
- CAF African Footballer of the Year
- BBC African Footballer of the Year
- Arab Footballer of the Year
- Premier League Golden Boot

MONTHLY AWARDS

- Premier League Player of the Month x3
- PFA Player of the Month x4
- Liverpool Player of the Month x7
- Liverpool Goal of the Month x6

WEEKLY AWARDS

- Champions League Player of the Week x2
- Champions League Goal of the Week x2

TEAM AWARDS

- PFA Team of the Year
- CAF Team of the Year

PLAYER PROFILES

DEJAN LOVREN

Date of birth: 5/7/1989

Birthplace: Zenica (Bosnia)

Squad Number: 6

Did You Know?
Lovren is one of only five Liverpool players to have played in a World Cup final

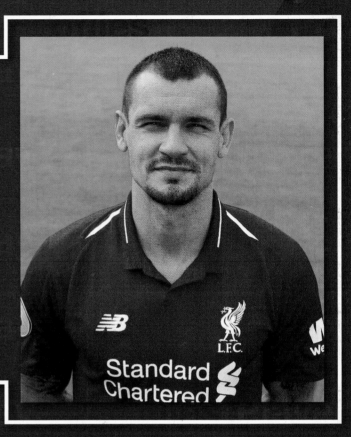

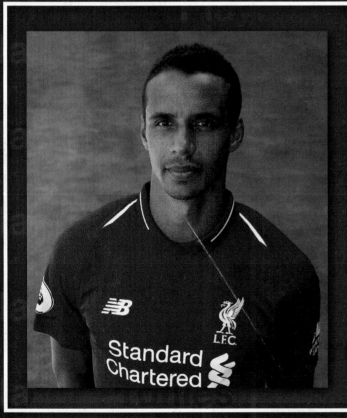

JOËL MATIP

Date of birth: 8/8/1991

Birthplace: Bochum (Germany)

Squad Number: 32

Did You Know?
During his time with former club Schalke, Matip was a DFB-Pokal (German Cup) winner in 2011

JOE GOMEZ

Date of birth: 23/5/1997

Birthplace:
Catford

Squad Number: 12

Did You Know?
Gomez was a member of the
England under-17 team that won
the European Championship in 2014

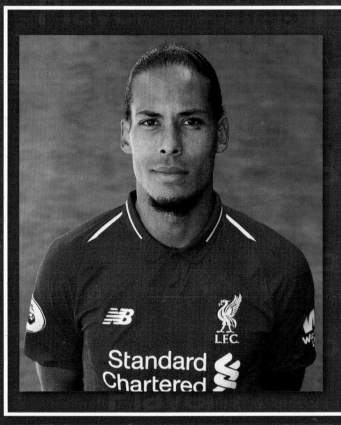

VIRGIL VAN DIJK

Date of birth: 8/7/1991

Birthplace:
Breda (Holland)

Squad Number: 4

Did You Know?
Van Dijk began his
career as a youth player
with Willem II, Sami
Hyypia's former club

A Knighthood for the King

The undisputed King of the Kop and a footballing legend in every sense, Kenny Dalglish won it all during a highly distinguished career as both a player and manager. Off the pitch he selflessly guided Liverpool through the tragedies of Heysel and Hillsborough, while his tireless and inspirational community work has made a powerful and lasting impact. As recognition for all that he's achieved it was announced in June 2018 that he was to be honoured with a knighthood.

Arise Sir Kenny Dalglish...

"Obviously it was for others with more education and knowledge than myself to decide whether or not I deserved a knighthood and it goes without saying that I am hugely grateful to them for the decision that they have made.

"All I can say is that from my own point of view I am definitely no more deserving of an accolade like this than Jock Stein, Bill Shankly and Bob Paisley were. I am just fortunate enough to be in the right place at the right time and I would like to dedicate this honour to them because without the standards that they set at Glasgow Celtic and Liverpool, individuals like myself would not have been able to thrive as much as we did.

"The most important thing to stress is that this honour is not a reflection of myself. It is a reflection of everyone who has played a part in my life and my career. Nobody achieves anything alone, especially in football, and in my case any success I have enjoyed has been due to the contributions made by my family, the players, coaches and managers that I was fortunate enough to work with and the supporters who backed me. This instance is no different.

"The enjoyment that I have derived from being involved in football for as long as I have is outstripped only by the sense that I've been hugely fortunate to have the right people around me at all times. None more so than my family whose support allowed me to focus on playing and managing, sometimes to the detriment of their own aspirations and ambitions. They share this honour as much as anyone else because without them none of this would have been possible."

DEBUT DELIGHT FOR VVD

What better way to mark your first appearance in a Liverpool shirt than by scoring a late winner in a cup-tie against your nearest and dearest rivals!

Well that's exactly how Virgil Van Dijk introduced himself to the Anfield crowd on a cold and wintry Friday night in January 2018.

The big Dutchman had been signed from Southampton earlier in the week and Jürgen Klopp had no hesitation pitching him straight into the white-hot atmosphere of a Merseyside derby.

The occasion was a televised third round FA Cup tie and Van Dijk took it all in his stride, providing a calm and reassuring presence at the heart of defence.

In the 84th minute, with the score tied at 1-1 and a replay looking increasingly likely, Liverpool's new number four then popped up at the opposite end to net with a towering header at the Kop end.

It was enough to clinch a memorable 2-1 victory and earn Virgil Van Dijk instant cult-status among the supporters.

HOMEGROWN HERO:
The Rise of Trent Alexander-Arnold

Trent Alexander-Arnold is living the dream and enjoying every minute of it.

A boyhood Liverpudlian who grew up in the shadow of Liverpool's West Derby training complex, Trent was one of the club's major success stories in 2017/18.

He's the latest Academy graduate to make his mark in the first team and, on the evidence of the progress made so far, he has all the attributes to become a permanent fixture in the Reds XI for a long time to come. Talented and level-headed, this young Scouser is a shining example for any aspiring footballer.

Alexander-Arnold initially joined Liverpool as a six-year old and worked his way through the ranks – impressing at every level – and captaining both the under-16 and under-18 teams.

Even at such an early age his ability was attracting admiring glances and former Liverpool captain Steven Gerrard confidently tipped him as first team player of the future.

A central midfielder turned right-back, his fine progress was rewarded with a surprise call-up to the senior side for a pre-season friendly away to Swindon in August 2015. Two months later he signed his first professional contract and within a year Trent Alexander-Arnold was knocking on the door of the first team squad.

After being named on the bench for the 2016/17 season opener away to Arsenal, his big moment finally arrived on the night of 25 October 2016 when, just two weeks after turning 18, he ran out at Anfield for his competitive first team debut against Tottenham in a League Cup tie at Anfield. As first starts go, it was certainly one to be proud of and although substituted midway through the second half, he left the field to a standing ovation.

Manager Jürgen Klopp clearly had a lot of faith in him. Alexander-Arnold completed the full 90 minutes at home to Leeds in the next round and then, in December, got his first taste of action in the Premier League as a late substitute away to Middlesbrough.

In January 2017, he made his FA Cup bow in the third round clash with Plymouth but the real proof of just how far he'd progressed came the following week when Klopp had no hesitation in handing him his first start in the Premier League – against Manchester United at Old Trafford.

In the heat of such a frenzied battle, an extremely accomplished performance was a further hint that he had what it takes to succeed at this level. Come the end of that campaign Alexander-Arnold had 12 first team appearances under his belt and was rewarded with a new long-term contact.

An impressive pre-season, coupled with an unfortunate injury to Nathaniel Clyne meant he began 2017/18 as a regular starter in Klopp's team and he fully grasped the opportunity.

Another milestone moment arrived when he scored his first senior goal – a stunning free-kick in the Champions League qualifier against Hoffenheim. Come the end of an unforgettable campaign he'd netted another two and more than tripled his amount of first team appearances.

The role he played in helping Liverpool reach the Champions League final took his game to a completely new level and enhanced his growing reputation even further. His subsequent call-up to England's 2018 World Cup squad therefore came as no surprise and was fully deserved.

Trent Alexander-Arnold has certainly come a long way in a short space of time. The club's reigning 'Young Player of the Year' has plenty to be proud about and, hopefully, should his development continue, an even brighter future lies ahead for him.

Neil Redfearn: Women's Manager

The summer of 2018 was one of change for Liverpool FC Women with some major changes in personnel – including a new manager, former professional footballer Neil Redfearn…

Neil, what is it that attracted you to the role of Liverpool Women's Manager?

The potential and the chance to be at the top level in women's football, giving my knowledge and ability to develop players at this level. It's a real opportunity and something I'm really relishing.

You're hugely experienced in the game – what else do you think you can offer as Liverpool Women's manager?

It's about the people we work with and how we develop them. It's easy to go in and look at a player but it's about developing and building a team. With the experience I've had of developing players, particularly young players, in my career as a coach I'm in a good place to do that.

How would you describe yourself as a manager?

Very positive. I'm very player-orientated; it's about them. It's about me getting the best out of them. But I want them to enjoy it and I want them to play with a smile on their face.

The landscape has changed a lot since Liverpool won back-to-back WSL titles. What do you think it's going to take to get the club challenging for silverware again?

It would be easy to try to go out and get all the best players and make a team that way. But not all the best teams contain the best players. It's about building a team, it's about working with the players, it's about having a structure and it's about having a foundation in place to have that success. This is what I'm going to try to do; we're going to come in and try to build towards that success.

The Liverpool Women's fan base is known for its vocal backing of the side. How much are you looking forward to giving them something to cheer about?

That's what it's all about: the people within your football club. Liverpool Women have got a fantastic following – they follow the girls up and down the country. We have had success and we need to try to get that back. We'll be doing everything we can to do that.

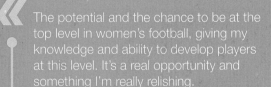

Purple Reign: Virgil Van Dijk and Xherdan Shaqiri celebrate with goalscorer Albert Moreno after the full-back netted in Liverpool's 5-0 pre-season victory over Napoli in Dublin.

LFC Award Winners

The annual LFC Players' Awards took place at Anfield in May 2018 and once again it was a huge success. Mo Salah, not surprisingly, stole the show but there was more than one winner on the night. Here's a complete list of who won what...

Player of the Season: Mohamed Salah
Players' Player of the Season: Mohamed Salah

Young Player of the Season:
Trent Alexander-Arnold

Goal of the Season: Alex
Oxlade-Chamberlain v Man
City (Champions League)

Academy Player of the Season:
Harry Wilson

LFC Ladies Player of the
Season: Gemma Bonner

LFC Ladies Players' Player
of the Season: Sophie Ingle

Lifetime Achievement
Award: Ian Callaghan

Outstanding Team
Achievement Award:
1978 European Cup
winners

Other winners on the night were....

Bill Shankly Community Award: Fans Supporting Foodbanks
Supporters' Club of the Season: New South Wales

Quiz Is Anfield

Put your Liverpool FC knowledge to the test with five rounds of questions on different subjects connected to the club...

CURRENT TEAM

- In what country was Mo Salah born?
- From which club did Liverpool sign Naby Keita?
- Who did Jürgen Klopp manage in the 2013 Champions League final?
- In which country did Trent Alexander-Arnold score his first Liverpool goal?
- Name the Liverpool defender who has played for Queen's Park and Dundee United?

TROPHIES

- Who did Liverpool beat when they last won the League Cup in 2012?
- How many times have Liverpool won the FA Cup?
- In which city have the Reds won the European Cup on two occasions?
- How many League Championships did Bob Paisley win as Liverpool manager?
- What trophy did Liverpool win for the first time by beating Hamburg over two legs in 1977?

FORMER PLAYERS

- Who left Liverpool in 1999 and went on to win the Champions League twice with Real Madrid?
- Who is the last Liverpool player to have scored a hat-trick against Manchester United?
- Which ex-Red's middle name is 'Everton'?
- Who scored on his Liverpool debut in February 2011, shortly after joining the club from Ajax?
- Name the Portuguese international who played for both Liverpool and Everton in a Merseyside derby during the 2001/02 season?

OPPONENTS

- Against which club did Liverpool suffer their heaviest Premier League defeat?
- For which club did Teddy Sheringham score the first goal against Liverpool in a Premier League game in August 1992?
- Name the only Welsh team Liverpool have faced in European competition?
- For which club did Julio Baptista once score four times at Anfield?
- Who were Liverpool knocked out of the FA Cup by in successive seasons in the 1980s?

ANFIELD

- Which Liverpool legend has a stand named after him at Anfield?
- In what year did supporters last stand on a terraced Kop?
- Which two countries played an international friendly at Anfield in June 2018?
- To the nearest thousand what is Anfield's record attendance?
- What famous TV show was broadcast from Anfield for the first time in August 1964?

Answers on P61.

PLAYER PROFILES

JAMES MILNER

Date of birth: 4/1/1986

Birthplace: Horsforth

Squad Number: 7

Did You Know?
Milner once held the record for being the youngest scorer in Premier League history

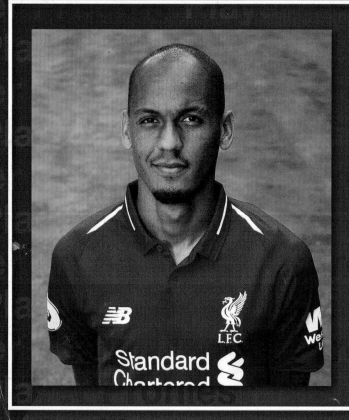

FABINHO

Date of birth: 23/10/1993

Birthplace:
Campinas (Brazil)

Squad Number: 3

Did You Know?
Fabinho's full name is Fabio Henrique Tavares

GEORGINIO WIJNALDUM

Date of birth: 11/11/1990

Birthplace:
Rotterdam (Holland)

Squad Number: 5

Did You Know?
Wijnaldum was Dutch Footballer
of the Year in 2015

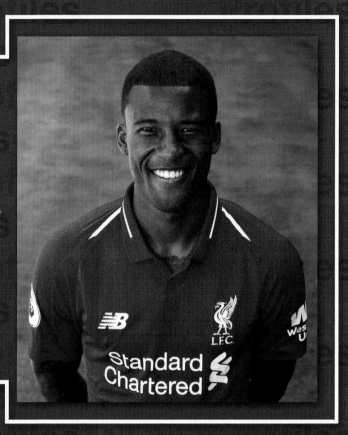

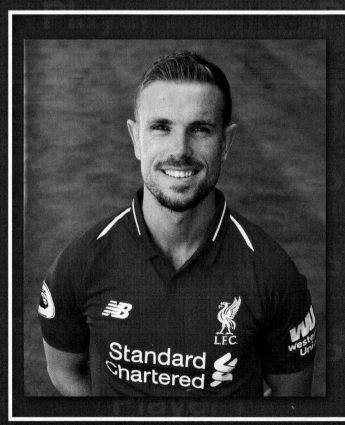

JORDAN HENDERSON

Date of birth: 17/6/1990

Birthplace: Sunderland

Squad Number: 14

Did You Know?
Henderson is Liverpool's current
longest-serving player, having
joined the club in 2011

WORDSEARCH

The names of every Liverpool manager (listed below) are hidden in this grid, search horizontally, vertically or diagonally, forwards or backwards, to find them...

L	R	L	X	N	N	A	W	B	E	N	I	T	E	Z
M	K	N	G	Y	N	T	N	V	R	M	M	B	G	H
B	T	Y	Y	N	A	N	O	S	G	D	O	H	P	O
L	G	B	E	H	N	K	F	F	R	C	Z	T	A	U
J	D	K	S	J	T	D	A	W	S	K	R	R	T	L
F	C	L	P	L	H	G	D	O	Y	O	F	O	T	L
M	E	X	E	Q	A	V	U	A	D	N	Y	W	E	I
W	V	Q	V	N	L	N	L	G	L	P	M	H	R	E
N	N	T	A	T	E	C	E	P	R	G	F	S	S	R
O	J	L	N	S	R	R	J	D	A	O	L	A	O	X
S	K	P	S	A	S	T	W	Z	W	I	L	I	N	L
T	V	P	B	L	D	Q	B	X	R	Y	S	Y	S	P
A	F	O	K	N	H	J	D	N	Q	M	K	L	A	H
W	P	L	K	M	C	Q	U	E	E	N	V	C	E	T
F	M	K	Y	L	K	N	A	H	S	Q	L	Q	J	Y

ASHWORTH

BARCLAY

BENITEZ

DALGLISH

EVANS

FAGAN

HODGSON

HOULLIER

KAY

KLOPP

MCKENNA

MCQUEEN

PAISLEY

PATTERSON

RODGERS

SHANKLY

SOUNESS

TAYLOR

WATSON

WELSH

42

Answers on P61.

Kop 1Os: Fill in the Blanks

The 10 Liverpool players who were voted Football Writers' Player of the Year prior to Mo Salah

1	2	3	4	5
6	7	8	9	10

The 10 teams Liverpool have played in a FA Cup final

1	2	3	4	5
6	7	8	9	10

The last 10 Liverpool players since the summer of 2004 to have scored a Premier League hat-trick prior to the 2018/19 season

1	2	3	4	5
6	7	8	9	10

The 10 French sides Liverpool have faced in European competition

1	2	3	4	5
6	7	8	9	10

The last 10 goalkeepers to play for Liverpool in the Premier League prior to Alisson Becker

1	2	3	4	5
6	7	8	9	10

The 10 Liverpool players to score for the club in a European Cup/Champions League final

1	2	3	4	5
6	7	8	9	10

Answers on P61.

LFC: A history in numbers

A statistical breakdown of Liverpool Football Club's illustrious history, from 1892-2018...

(all player/match related stats are for competitive first team games only and are up to and including the end of the 2017/18 season)

5632	matches played
2771	wins
1525	defeats
1341	draws

PERSONNEL

741	players
44	captains (on a permanent basis)
20	different permanent managers (including secretary/managers)

GOALS

9743	scored
6566	conceded
449	different scorers
191	own goals for
148	own goals against
931	debutant goalscorers
241	hat-tricks

PENALTIES

504	scored
198	missed
18	shoot-outs

TROPHIES

18	League titles
5	European Cups
7	FA Cups
3	UEFA Cups
8	League Cups
3	European Super Cups
1	Screen Sport Super Cup
15	Charity Shields
4	Second Division titles
1	Lancashire League title
39	Liverpool Senior Cups
18	Reserve League titles
3	FA Youth Cups

INDIVIDUAL AWARDS

1	European Player of the Year
7	PFA Players of the Year
13	Football Writers' Players of the Year
11	Managers of the Year
5	PFA Young Players of the Year
2	European Golden Boots
9	First Division/Premier League top scorers

MISCELLANEOUS

1	home ground
55	different countries played in around the world (including friendlies)
270	supporters' clubs around the world

KITS

2	different coloured home shirts
10	different coloured away/3rd shirts
5	shirt sponsors

Anfield Anagrams

Rearrange the letters in these words to reveal a past or present Liverpool player...

1 Baned Resort Worn

2 Thin Jason

3 Sesame Surgeon

4 Roman Basil

5 Halo Sam

6 Batter Chinese Ink

7 Leg Drainage

8 Insect Love

9 Scab Origin

10 Harrier Jam Cage

Answers on P61.

ROBERTO FIRMINO:
Anfield's Samba Star

Since joining Liverpool from Hoffenheim during the summer of 2015, Roberto Firmino has firmly established himself as one of the most exciting talents in world football and one of the most popular players currently at the club...

Why are you and Liverpool such a good match?

I think it is a cycle of friendship inside this football club. Everything fits in the best possible way. My teammates are fantastic and I am very grateful to be able to play with them at this club.

The engine is how Jürgen Klopp describes you... (what do you think about that)?

I think he is right when he says that! I am really an engine – I enjoy helping my team and I love to give my best all the time. I play every match without leaving anything behind and I hope I can continue moving forward playing in this way to help my team.

How influential has the manager been in bringing you to the level you're at now?

Yes, of course. The manager helped me a lot after he arrived here. The manager coming to the football club was not only good for me, but for the whole team. We've grown a lot and now we are showing that with the results on the pitch.

Your fellow forwards...Sadio Mané and Mohamed Salah. What's it like playing alongside those two?

Exceptional, both of them. They are excellent footballers with a lot of quality and I am grateful to play beside them. The whole team is doing a very good job on the pitch and everything is coming together in the correct manner.

Do you feel the qualities each of you possess complement each other and bring out the best in each other?

Yes, of course. Every day our relationship gets better and better and then in the games, we apply what we've worked on in training before. I hope that we can continue in this way, or even improve to become better.

2017/18 was your best ever season in terms of goals – but do you feel there's more to come for you?

Yes. I want more and more all the time. I am a stubborn boy and don't like to lose! I hope to work even harder to achieve good things that are yet to come.

Your celebrations are a big talking point too, how do you come up with them?

The day before, I sometimes think about what I'll do if I score, although my focus is always on the match ahead. Sometimes the celebration just comes naturally, but sometimes I plan ahead and have something in my mind to do if I score.

A lot of people think Sadio likes to copy your celebrations... what's your opinion?

I think so, too! I have seen a few videos of his celebrations. I think he has copied Coutinho in the past and now he is trying to copy me.

What do you believe the team can achieve in the future?

We all know how big Liverpool Football Club is. It is a club with a lot of tradition, so I hope to continue with the whole team going forward, dreaming aloud and aiming very high. Hopefully we will be able to win titles, that's the most important thing for us.

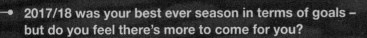

Tell us about your relationship with the Liverpool fans...

I love the fans. Every time I go into the city centre and see the fans, they always greet me and I feel very well here in the city. The fans are fantastic to me.

How does it make you feel when you hear them chant your name?

It is fantastic. It is the result of my hard work, the work I do on the pitch with the whole team. It is fantastic to hear it because it gives me more energy to give my very best on the pitch.

Finally, what is your message to the Liverpool fans?

I love to play for Liverpool FC. The fans are excellent and fantastic in how they support us all the way. They support us throughout the games and the work they do during the match is beautiful.

PLAYER PROFILES

ADAM LALLANA

Date of birth: 10/5/1988

Birthplace: St Albans

Squad Number: 20

Did You Know?
While still a Southampton player Lallana was named in the PFA Premier League team of the season for 2013/14

ALEX OXLADE-CHAMBERLAIN

Date of birth: 15/8/1993

Birthplace: Portsmouth

Squad Number: 21

Did You Know?
Oxlade-Chamberlain's dad Mark was also a professional footballer and so too is his brother Christian

NABY KEITA

Date of birth: 10/2/1995

Birthplace: Conakry (Guinea)

Squad Number: 8

Did You Know?
Keita is only the second player from Guinea to play for Liverpool, following in the footsteps of Titi Camara

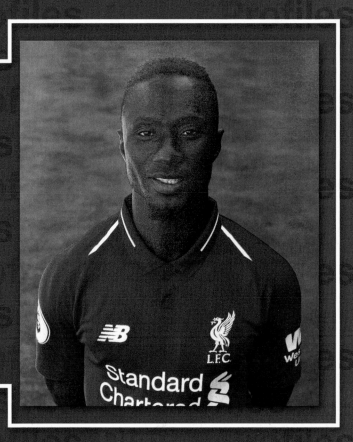

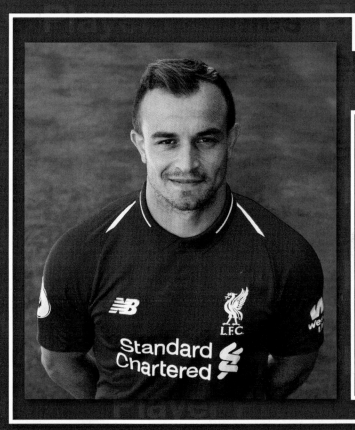

XHERDAN SHAQIRI

Date of birth: 10/10/1991

Birthplace: Gjilan (Kosovo)

Squad Number: 23

Did You Know?
Shaqiri was a member of the Bayern Munich squad that defeated Jürgen Klopp's Borussia Dortmund in the 2013 Champions League final

WORLD CUP REDS

Liverpool had eight representatives at the 2018 World Cup in Russia and it was a tournament of mixed emotions for our boys out there...

Runner-up
Dejan Lovren (Croatia)

Lovren became only the fifth Liverpool player to appear in a World Cup final – following in the footsteps of Roger Hunt, Dietmar Hamann, Dirk Kuyt and Fernando Torres. The Reds defender featured in every game of the tournament for Croatia as they topped their group and then defeated Denmark and Russia on penalties before eliminating England in the semi-final. A 4-2 defeat to France in the final eventually ended Lovren's dream of becoming a world champion but it was a tournament from which he emerged with great credit and one he'll never forget.

3rd place
Simon Mignolet (Belgium)

Belgium were one of the outstanding teams of the 2018 World Cup and succumbed only to eventual winners France in the semi-final. Mignolet had to make do though with a place on the bench for all seven games due to the fine form of Chelsea's Thibout Courtois.

4th Place Jordan Henderson & Trent Alexander-Arnold (England)

Henderson was an integral part of England's best World Cup performance since 1990. The Liverpool captain earned rave reviews for his midfield performances as the Three Lions progressed to the last four, featuring in five of the seven games. For Alexander-Arnold, a late addition to the squad, this tournament was all about the experience and although he spent the majority of his time on the bench he did start in the final group game against Belgium.

Quarter-finalist
Roberto Firmino (Brazil)

Most Liverpool supporters will be in agreement that Firmino was under-used by Brazil at Russia 2018. Despite enjoying a great season for his club, his country opted not to start him in any of their five World Cup games. The Liverpool number nine came off the bench three times and scored one goal, netting just two minutes after entering the action in the round of 16 tie against Mexico.

Group Stage
Mo Salah (Egypt)

After missing the opening game – a 1-0 defeat to Uruguay – Salah returned as Egypt took on the hosts in Saint Petersburg and scored from the penalty spot. Unfortunately, it proved only to be a consolation goal as Russia ran out 3-1 winners, a result that deemed Egypt's final group game meaningless in terms of qualification to the knockout phase. Against Saudi Arabia Salah netted again but Egypt's miserable tournament was completed with a 2-1 defeat.

Group Stage
Sadio Mané (Senegal)

Mané proudly captained his country in Russia but suffered group stage disappointment too. Following a 2-1 victory over Poland in the opening game, Mané scored Senegal's first goal in a 2-2 draw with Japan and was voted man-of-the match. A draw against Colombia in the final game would have been enough to see them through to the last 16 but a 1-0 defeat consigned Senegal to an early exit.

Group Stage
Marko Grujic (Serbia)

Grujic was an unused substitute in all three of Serbia's group games. Despite winning their opening game against Costa Rica subsequent defeats to Switzerland and Brazil meant they failed to advance.

Packing Out The Big House

Liverpool's 2018 summer tour of the US was deemed a huge success in more ways than one.

Not only did the Reds warm up for the new season with impressive victories over Premier League rivals Manchester City and Manchester United, they also played in front of the biggest crowd in the club's history.

After games in Charlotte (v Borussia Dortmund) and New Jersey (v City), Jürgen Klopp's side headed west to round off their stay Stateside with a match against United at the Michigan Stadium in Ann Arbor.

Known locally as 'The Big House', it's the largest football stadium in America and a remarkable 101,254 were in attendance to see Liverpool run out comprehensive 4-1 winners – the highlight of which was Xherdan Shaqiri's spectacular overhead kick that completed the scoring.

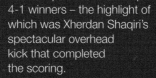

Liverpool's Latest Great Scot

The presence of Andrew Robertson in Liverpool's first team is a reassuring sight. Not only did the popular full-back prove an instant hit during his debut season at the club, he also became the latest in a long line of talented Scotsmen to ply their trade in a red shirt. And for those who know their history, that can only be a good omen.

Liverpool Football Club has a long and successful association with players born north of the border.

It dates way back to 1892, when the club's first ever mass recruitment drive resulted in a flurry of Scots being signed up. This fledgling Liverpool eleven famously became known as 'The Team of Macs' and a precedent had been set.

In the years that followed most victorious Liverpool teams contained at least one player of Scottish heritage and many of them are now regarded among the greatest to have ever graced the red shirt.

In 1901 **Alex Raisbeck** captained Liverpool to a first League title, while four decades later flying winger **Billy Liddell** exerted such an influence on the side that it was often renamed 'Liddellpool' in his honour.

During the 1960s, **Bill Shankly**'s resurrection of the club was built around **Ian St John** and **Ron Yeats** and the foundations they helped lay were later built upon by a team featuring the triple European Cup winning trio of **Kenny Dalglish**, **Alan Hansen** and **Graeme Souness**.

The versatile, but often unsung, **Steve Nicol** later joined them as a serial trophy winner at Anfield, while an ageing **Gary McAllister** revived the tradition at the turn of the century by inspiring the Reds to an historic cup treble.

> **What Robertson said upon joining Liverpool:**
>
> *"There's not many, if any, more special clubs than Liverpool. When you grow up as a kid you dream of playing with big clubs such as Liverpool and to make that a reality is a dream come true for me."*

What Jürgen Klopp said when signing Robertson:

"For Andrew this is another big step on what has been quite an incredible personal journey in a very short space of time. I know our environment will benefit him and help him push himself even more than he has already. This is a player who does not limit his ambition."

FACT-FILE

Born: 11 March 1994

Birthplace: Glasgow

Previous clubs:
Queen's Park,
Dundee United, Hull City

International debut:
5 March 2014 v Poland

International caps: 17

International goals: 2

International stats correct up to and including end of the 2017/18 season.

Kenny Dalglish's verdict on Anfield's latest Scottish star...

"Andy has been fantastic ever since he came into the team. Everyone in Scotland should be very, very proud of him. Andy's a quality player. He has pace, his final ball is excellent and he plays with his heart on his sleeve. It gives me a lot of satisfaction to see him flying the flag for Scotland."

Since then there had been a dearth of Scottish talent at Liverpool and when **Andrew Robertson** was signed from Hull City in the summer of 2017 he became the first Scot at the club since Charlie Adam played his last Liverpool game five years before.

It took just one game, however – his debut at home to Crystal Palace in August 2017 – for Robertson to win over the Liverpool fans and he quickly became a huge crowd favourite, impressing with his high-energy approach, never-say-die attitude, tenacious tackling and the pinpoint accuracy of his crossing.

His subsequent performances during a campaign in which he made 30 appearances and played a key role in Liverpool's run to the Champions League final have raised hopes that the club has another great Scot in its ranks.

Did you know?

- Robertson was a boyhood Celtic fan and a season-ticket holder at Parkhead until he broke into the Queens Park first team

- He had also been on Celtic's books as a schoolboy but was released when he was 15

- While playing as an amateur for Queen's Park, he also worked part-time for the Scottish FA at Hampden Park and on the tills at Marks & Spencer

- He scored his first senior international goal against England in November 2014

- During his time at Hull he twice suffered relegation and once celebrated promotion

- He broke his scoring duck for Liverpool in the final Premier League game of the 2017/18 season in a 4-0 home win over Brighton

Andrew Robertson is the latest in a long line of illustrious Scotsmen to play for Liverpool. Here's just a few of them...

LIVERPOOL'S ALL-TIME SCOTTISH XI

YOUNGER

NICOL   YEATS   HANSEN   MACKINLAY

SOUNESS   RAISBECK   MCALLISTER

ST JOHN   DALGLISH   LIDDELL

TOMMY YOUNGER
Birthplace: Edinburgh. Liverpool's first choice 'keeper in the late fifties and Scotland's number one at the 1958 World Cup.

STEVE NICOL
Birthplace: Ayrshire. Extremely versatile player who was an unsung member of the great Liverpool team of the mid to late 1980s.

RON YEATS
Birthplace: Aberdeen. The cornerstone of Bill Shankly's first great Liverpool team and the first Reds' captain to lift the FA Cup.

ALEX RAISBECK
Birthplace: Stirlingshire. Liverpool's first title-winning captain and arguably the club's first genuine superstar.

DONALD MACKINLAY
Birthplace: Newton Mearns. Long-serving defender who captained Liverpool to back-to-back league titles in the 1920s.

BILLY LIDDELL
Birthplace: Townhill. Legendary winger of the post-war era and the ultimate idol to a generation of Liverpool supporters.

IAN ST JOHN
Birthplace: Motherwell. A key figure in the club's revival in the 1960s and scorer of the goal that won Liverpool's first FA Cup.

KENNY DALGLISH
Birthplace: Glasgow. Liverpool's greatest-ever player and one of the club's most successful managers.

ALAN HANSEN
Birthplace: Sauchie. Double-winning captain of 1986 and one of the finest centre-backs to ever play the game.

GRAEME SOUNESS
Birthplace: Edinburgh. Treble-winning captain of 1984 and Liverpool's midfield general during its most glorious spell.

GARY MCALLISTER
Birthplace: Motherwell. Experienced midfielder who helped Liverpool to a unique cup treble in 2001.

A Liver Bird on Our Crest

The Liver Bird has, and always will be, universally known as the famous emblem of Liverpool Football Club. It has featured on every club crest we've ever had and taken on various guises through the years. Here's how it's evolved over time…

What is a Liver Bird?

The Liver Bird is a mythical creature – believed to be a cross between a cormorant and an eagle – and it derives from medieval times, when King John granted the city of Liverpool its first charter in 1207.

This is Liverpool FC's first known club crest and it was used up until the Second World War. It was never worn on a shirt but it was a distinctive feature on all club correspondence during the first 50-plus years of the Liverpool history. It was also prominent as the masthead on the front cover of the matchday programme in the late 1930s.

As with the above, this crest never appeared on the shirt but was used for administrative and merchandise purposes between 1946 and 1970. It briefly re-appeared in 1981 on the front cover of the European Cup final against Real Madrid in Paris.

This shield-style crest – of which there were a number of slightly different versions – was introduced in the early 1970s and remained popular through to the early 1990s. Again, it was predominantly used for administration and merchandise but in 1987 it replaced the solitary Liver Bird emblem that had previously adorned the shirt and remained until 1992.

To commemorate the club's centenary in 1992 Liverpool's crest was given its first official makeover in over two decades and in addition to referencing the years a reproduction of the top of the iconic Shankly Gates was introduced.

After just one season the 'centenary' crest underwent a few subtle changes, notably the introduction of the Hillsborough flames at either side.

At the turn of the century a new crest was unveiled and it's the one we see around Anfield today. It didn't alter much in terms of design but was given a more modern look and feel. As part of the club's 125th birthday celebrations in 2017/18 dates were added to commemorate the anniversary before the crest returned in its former guise for the current campaign.

Spot The Difference

Take a close look at the two pictures below and see if you can spot the 10 differences...

Answers on P61.

MISSING MEN

We've blanked out the faces of two players from the following team line-ups, can you name them?

Porto (a) 14 February 2018

1
....
....

2
....
....

Manchester City (a) 10 April 2018

3
....
....

4
....
....

AS Roma (a) 2 May 2018

5
....
....

6
....
....

Answers on P61.

PLAYER PROFILES

MOHAMED SALAH

Date of birth: 15/6/1992

Birthplace: Basyoun (Egypt)

Squad Number: 11

Did You Know?
No player has scored more goals in a debut season for Liverpool than Salah in 2017/18

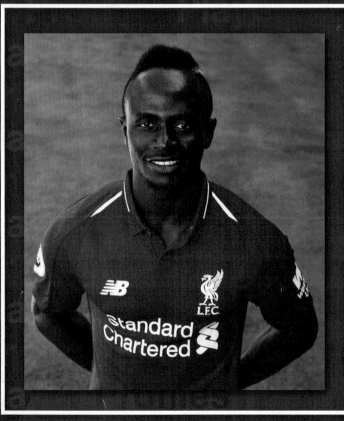

SADIO MANÉ

Date of birth: 10/4/1992

Birthplace: Sédhiou (Senegal)

Squad Number: 10

Did You Know?
Mané is one of just ten players to have scored for Liverpool in a European Cup/Champions League final

ROBERTO FIRMINO

Date of birth: 2/10/1991

Birthplace: Maceió (Brazil)

Squad Number: 9

Did You Know?
Firmino hails from the same city as the legendary Mario Zagallo, a three-time Brazilian World Cup winner

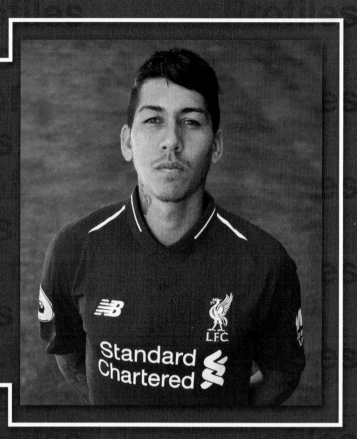

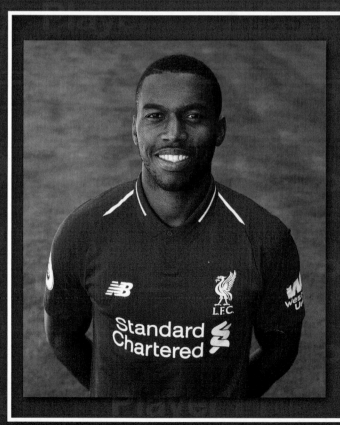

DANIEL STURRIDGE

Date of birth: 1/9/1989

Birthplace: Birmingham

Squad Number: 15

Did You Know?
Sturridge was on the losing side for Manchester City against Liverpool in the 2006 FA Youth Cup final

LFC Shirt Competition

Last year's winner James with his signed shirt!

Who was Liverpool's top goalscorer in the 2017/18 season?

A Mo Salah

B Sadio Mané

C Roberto Firmino

Entry is by email only. Only one entry per contestant. Please enter LFC SHIRT followed by either A, B or C in the subject line of an email. In the body of the email, please include your full name, address, postcode, email address and phone number and send to: frontdesk@grangecommunications. co.uk by Friday 29th March 2019.

Terms and Conditions

1) The closing date for this competition is Friday the 29th March 2019 at midnight. Entries received after that time will not be counted.

2) Information on how to enter and on the prizes form part of these conditions.

3) Entry is open to those residing in the UK only. If entrants are under 18, consent from a parent or guardian must be obtained and the parent or guardian must agree to these terms and conditions.

4) This competition is not open to employees or their relatives of Liverpool FC. Any such entries will be invalid.

5) The start date for entries is 31st October 2018 at 4pm.

6) Entries must be strictly in accordance with these terms and conditions. Any entry not in strict accordance with these terms and conditions will be deemed to be invalid and no prizes will be awarded in respect of such entry. By entering, all entrants will be deemed to accept these rules.

7) One (1) lucky winner will win a 2018/2019 season signed football shirt.

8) The prize is non-transferable and no cash alternative will be offered. Entry is by email only. Only one entry per contestant. Please enter LFC SHIRT followed by either A, B or C in the subject line of an email. In the body of the email, please include your full name, address, postcode, email address and phone number and send to: frontdesk@grangecommunications.co.uk by Friday 29th March 2019.

9) The winner will be picked at random. The winner will be contacted within 72 hours of the closing date. Details of the winners can be requested after this time from the address below.

10) Entries must not be sent in through agents or third parties. No responsibility can be accepted for lost, delayed, incomplete, or for electronic entries or winning notifications that are not received or delivered. Any such entries will be deemed void.

11) The winners shall have 72 hours to claim their prize once initial contact has been made by the Promoter. Failure to respond may result in forfeiture of the prize.

12) The Promoter reserves the right to withdraw or amend the promotion as necessary due to circumstances outside its reasonable control. The Promoter's decision on all matters is final and no correspondence will be entered into.

13) The Promoter (or any third party nominated by the Promoter) may use the winner's name and image and their comments relating to the prize for future promotional, marketing and publicity purposes in any media worldwide without notice or without any fee being paid.

14) Liverpool Football Club's decision is final, no correspondence will be entered in to. Except in respect of death or personal injury resulting from any negligence of the Club, neither The Liverpool Football Club nor any of its officers, employees or agents shall be responsible for (whether in tort, contract or otherwise):

(i) any loss, damage or injury to you and/or any guest or to any property belonging to you or any guest in connection with this competition and/or the prize, resulting from any cause whatsoever;

(ii) for any loss of profit, loss of use, loss of opportunity or any indirect, economic or consequential losses whatsoever;

15) This competition shall be governed by English law.

16) Promoter: Grange Communications, 22 Great King Street, Edinburgh EH3 6QH.

Answers

P39 Quiz Is Anfield

Current Team
Egypt
Red Bull Leipzig
Borussia Dortmund
Germany
Andrew Robertson
Trophies
Cardiff City
Seven
Rome
Six
Super Cup
Former Players
Steve McManaman
Dirk Kuyt

Mark Walters
Luis Suarez
Abel Xavier
Opponents
Stoke City
Nottingham Forest
Total Network Solutions (TNS)
Arsenal
Brighton & Hove Albion
Anfield
Sir Kenny Dalglish
1994
Brazil & Croatia
62,000
Match of the Day

P43 Kop 10s

Ian Callaghan, Emlyn Hughes, Kevin Keegan, Kenny Dalglish, Terry McDermott, Ian Rush, John Barnes, Steve Nicol, Steven Gerrard, Luis Suarez

Burnley, Arsenal, Leeds United, Newcastle United, Manchester United, Everton, Wimbledon, Sunderland, West Ham United, Chelsea

Milan Baros, Peter Crouch, Fernando Torres, Steven Gerrard, Yossi Benayoun, Dirk Kuyt, Maxi Rodriguez, Luis Suarez, Daniel Sturridge, Mo Salah

St Etienne, Auxerre, Paris St Germain, Strasbourg, Marseille, Monaco, Bordeaux, Toulouse, Lyon, Lille

Loris Karius, Simon Mignolet, Adam Bogdan, Danny Ward, Brad Jones, Pepe Reina, Alexander Doni, Jerzy Dudek, Daniele Padelli, Scott Carson

Terry McDermott, Tommy Smith, Phil Neal, Kenny Dalglish, Alan Kennedy, Steven Gerrard, Xabi Alonso, Vladimir Smicer, Dirk Kuyt, Sadio Mane

P56 Spot The Difference

P42 Wordsearch

L	R	L	X	N	N	A	W	B	E	N	I	T	E	Z
M	K	N	G	Y	N	T	N	V	R	M	M	B	G	H
B	T	Y	Y	N	A	N	O	S	G	D	O	H	P	O
L	G	B	E	H	N	K	F	F	R	C	Z	T	A	U
J	D	K	S	J	T	D	A	W	S	K	R	R	T	L
F	C	L	P	L	H	G	D	O	Y	O	F	O	T	L
M	E	X	E	Q	A	V	U	A	D	N	Y	W	E	I
W	V	Q	V	N	L	N	L	G	L	P	M	H	R	E
N	N	T	A	T	E	C	E	P	R	G	F	S	S	R
O	J	L	N	S	R	R	J	D	A	O	L	A	O	X
S	K	P	S	A	S	T	W	Z	W	I	L	I	N	L
T	V	P	B	L	D	Q	B	X	R	Y	S	Y	S	P
A	F	O	K	N	H	J	D	N	Q	M	K	L	A	H
W	P	L	K	M	C	Q	U	E	E	N	V	C	E	T
F	M	K	Y	L	K	N	A	H	S	Q	L	Q	J	Y

P45 Anfield Anagrams

1. Andrew Robertson
2. Ian St John
3. Graeme Souness
4. Milan Baros
5. Mo Salah
6. Christian Benteke
7. Daniel Agger
8. Steve Nicol
9 Igor Biscan
10. Jamie Carragher

P57 Missing Men

Porto (a) 14 February 2018
1. Van Dijk (back row 3rd from right)
2. Milner (front row 1st from left)

Manchester City (a) 10 April 2018
3. Firmino (back row 2nd from left)
4. Robertson (front row 2nd from right)

AS Roma (a) 2 May 2018
5. Lovren (back row 2nd from left)
6. Wijnaldum (front row far right)

Where's Mighty Red?

Mighty Red joined the fans for this match.
Can you find Mighty Red in the crowd?